Master Maths at Home

Addition and Subtraction

Scan the QR code to help your child's learning at home.

DK | MATHS NO PROBLEM!

mastermathsathome.com

How to use this book

Maths — No Problem! created Master Maths at Home to help children develop fluency in the subject and a rich understanding of core concepts.

Key features of the Master Maths at Home books include:

- Carefully designed lessons that provide structure, but also allow flexibility in how they're used.

- Speech bubbles containing content designed to spark diverse conversations, with many discussion points that don't have obvious 'right' or 'wrong' answers.

- Rich illustrations that will guide children to a discussion of shapes and units of measurement, allowing them to make connections to the wider world around them.

- Exercises that allow a flexible approach and can be adapted to suit any child's cognitive or functional ability.

- Clearly laid-out pages that encourage children to practise a range of higher-order skills.

- A community of friendly and relatable characters who introduce each lesson and come along as your child progresses through the series.

You can see more guidance on how to use these books at **mastermathsathome.com**.

We're excited to share all the ways you can learn maths!

Copyright © 2022 Maths — No Problem!

Maths — No Problem!
mastermathsathome.com
www.mathsnoproblem.com
hello@mathsnoproblem.com

First published in Great Britain in 2022 by
Dorling Kindersley Limited
One Embassy Gardens, 8 Viaduct Gardens, London SW11 7BW
A Penguin Random House Company

The authorised representative in the EEA is Dorling Kindersley
Verlag GmbH. Amulfstr. 124, 80636 Munich, Germany

10 9 8 7 6 5 4 3 2 1
001–327087–Jan/22

A CIP catalogue record for this book is available from the British Library.

ISBN: 978-0-24153-932-3
Printed and bound in the UK

For the curious
www.dk.com

This book was made with Forest Stewardship Council™ certified paper – one small step in DK's commitment to a sustainable future. For more information go to www.dk.com/our-green-pledge

Acknowledgements
The publisher would like to thank the authors and consultants Andy Psarianos, Judy Hornigold, Adam Gifford and Dr Anne Hermanson.

The Castledown typeface has been used with permission from the Colophon Foundry.

Contents

Ruby   Elliott   Amira   Charles   Lulu   Sam   Oak   Holly   Ravi   Emma   Jacob   Hannah

Place value

Starter

How many stickers does Hannah have altogether?

Example

We can use place-value counters to show the number of stickers.

Each packet has 1000 stickers.

We say one thousand.

1000

100

10

1

These represent 1000, 10 and 1.

4

 There are 5 thousands, 6 hundreds, 1 ten and 5 ones.

 We say five thousand, six hundred and fifteen.

Altogether, Hannah has 5615 stickers.

Practice

Count and write the numbers in words and in numerals.

The first one has been done for you.

1 1000 1000 100 100 10 10 1 1
1000 100 100 10 1 1
100 1

three thousand, five hundred and thirty-five

3535

2 1000 1000 100 100 10 10 1 1
1000 1000 100 100 10 10 1 1
1000 1000 100 1 1
1000

3 1000 1000 100 100 10 10 1 1
1000 1000 100 10 10 1 1
10 10 1 1
1

4 1000 100 100 10 10 1 1
100 100 10 1 1
100 100 1 1
100

Comparing and ordering numbers

7   1   9   3

Arrange the digits to create the greatest possible number and the smallest possible number.

Example

thousands	hundreds	tens	ones
1000 1000 1000 1000 1000 1000 1000 1000 1000	100 100 100 100 100 100 100	10 10 10	1
9	7	3	1

We need to put the greatest digit in the thousands place to make the greatest number. The greatest digit is 9.

9731 is the greatest number we can make.

We need to put the second greatest digit in the hundreds place, the third greatest number in the tens place and the smallest number in the ones place.

To make the smallest number, we need to put the smallest digit in the thousands place and then the next smallest digits in the hundreds, tens and ones places.

thousands	hundreds	tens	ones
1000	100 100 100	10 10 10 10 10 10 10	1 1 1 1 1 1 1 1 1
1	3	7	9

The smallest number we can make is 1379.

The greatest number we can make from the digit cards is 9731 and the smallest number is 1379.

Practice

1 Arrange from smallest to greatest.

(a) 4680, 5762, 3598, 1298

(b) 3784, 3893, 3779, 3778

☐ , ☐ , ☐ , ☐   ☐ , ☐ , ☐ , ☐

2 Arrange from greatest to smallest.

(a) 3112, 2875, 2956, 4012

(b) 5479, 5542, 5601, 5543

☐ , ☐ , ☐ , ☐   ☐ , ☐ , ☐ , ☐

Adding without renaming

On Saturday, 2463 people visited the museum.
On Sunday, 3135 people visited the museum.

How many people visited the museum over the weekend?

Example

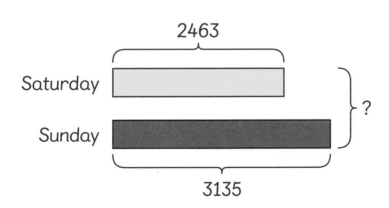

We need to add to find the sum.

8

1000 1000	100 100	10 10	1 1
	100 100	10 10	1
		10 10	
1000 1000	100	10 10	1 1
1000		10	1 1
			1

Step 1   Add the ones.
Step 2   Add the tens.
Step 3   Add the hundreds.
Step 4   Add the thousands.

```
    2   4   6   3
+   3   1   3   5
─────────────────
    5   5   9   8
─────────────────
```

5598 people visited the museum over the weekend.

1   Add.

(a)
```
    4   6   3   8
+   3   2   4   1
─────────────────
  [ ][ ][ ][ ]
```

(b)
```
    7   2   4   3
+   2   7   4   6
─────────────────
  [ ][ ][ ][ ]
```

(c)
```
    2   0   2   3
+   6   3   2   5
─────────────────
  [ ][ ][ ][ ]
```

(d)
```
    8   4   2   3
+   1   5   1   6
─────────────────
  [ ][ ][ ][ ]
```

(e)
```
    6   1   5   3
+   3   8   4   6
─────────────────
  [ ][ ][ ][ ]
```

(f)
```
    3   2   7   5
+   5   6   1   3
─────────────────
  [ ][ ][ ][ ]
```

2   (a)   In Canada, the drive from Vancouver to Toronto is 4411 km.
The drive from Toronto to Moncton is an additional 1532 km.
What is the driving distance from Vancouver to Moncton?

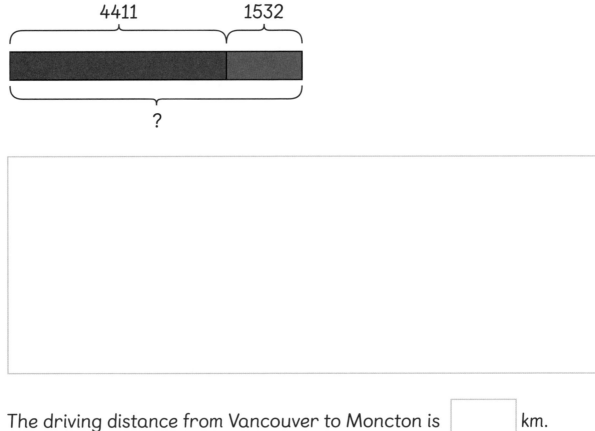

The driving distance from Vancouver to Moncton is ☐ km.

(b)   The drive from Moncton to Mirabel is an additional 1035 km.
What is the total driving distance from Vancouver to Mirabel?

The total driving distance from Vancouver to Mirabel is ☐ km.

3 Use all of these digits to make two 4-digit numbers for each question.

| 5 | 4 | 4 | 4 | 3 | 3 | 3 | 2 |

(a) Find two numbers that have the greatest possible sum.

```
    ☐ ☐ ☐ ☐
  + ☐ ☐ ☐ ☐
  ─────────────
    ☐ ☐ ☐ ☐
```

(b) Find two other numbers that have the greatest possible sum.

```
    ☐ ☐ ☐ ☐
  + ☐ ☐ ☐ ☐
  ─────────────
    ☐ ☐ ☐ ☐
```

(c) Find two numbers that have the smallest possible sum.

```
    ☐ ☐ ☐ ☐
  + ☐ ☐ ☐ ☐
  ─────────────
    ☐ ☐ ☐ ☐
```

(d) Find two other numbers that have the smallest possible sum.

```
    ☐ ☐ ☐ ☐
  + ☐ ☐ ☐ ☐
  ─────────────
    ☐ ☐ ☐ ☐
```

Adding with renaming (part 1)

Starter

A sofa costs £2325 and an armchair costs £1549.
How much do the sofa and armchair cost altogether?

£2325

£1549

Example

£2325   £1549

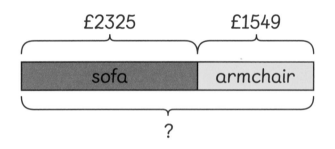

| sofa | armchair |

?

Find the sum of 2325 and 1549.

Step 1   Add the ones.
5 ones and 9 ones = 14 ones
Rename the ones.
14 ones = 1 ten and 4 ones

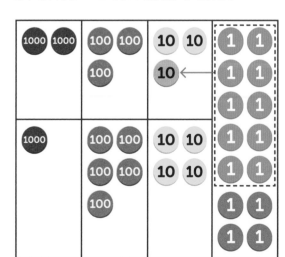

$$
\begin{array}{r}
2\ \ 3\ \ \overset{1}{2}\ \ 5 \\
+\ 1\ \ 5\ \ 4\ \ 9 \\
\hline
4 \\
\hline
\end{array}
$$

Step 2   Add the tens.
2 tens + 4 tens + 1 ten = 7 tens

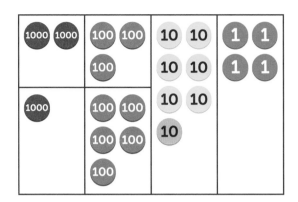

$$
\begin{array}{r}
2\ \ 3\ \ {}^{1}2\ \ 5 \\
+\ 1\ \ 5\ \ 4\ \ 9 \\
\hline
7\ \ 4
\end{array}
$$

Step 3   Add the hundreds.
3 hundreds + 5 hundreds = 8 hundreds

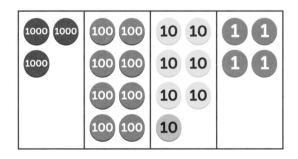

$$
\begin{array}{r}
2\ \ 3\ \ {}^{1}2\ \ 5 \\
+\ 1\ \ 5\ \ 4\ \ 9 \\
\hline
8\ \ 7\ \ 4
\end{array}
$$

Step 4   Add the thousands.
2 thousands + 1 thousand = 3 thousands

$$
\begin{array}{r}
2\ \ 3\ \ {}^{1}2\ \ 5 \\
+\ 1\ \ 5\ \ 4\ \ 9 \\
\hline
3\ \ 8\ \ 7\ \ 4
\end{array}
$$

2325 + 1549 = 3874
Altogether, the sofa and the armchair cost £3874.

1 Add.

(a)
```
   3  2  4  7
+  2  5  4  6
  ▢  ▢  ▢  ▢
```

(b)
```
   1  4  3  5
+  5  3  5  6
  ▢  ▢  ▢  ▢
```

(c)
```
   5  4  3  6
+  1  0  2  8
  ▢  ▢  ▢  ▢
```

(d)
```
   1  1  0  6
+  2  1  5  6
  ▢  ▢  ▢  ▢
```

(e)
```
   8  2  6  1
+  1  6  2  9
  ▢  ▢  ▢  ▢
```

(f)
```
   1  3  3  9
+  8  5  5  1
  ▢  ▢  ▢  ▢
```

(g)
```
   1  1  1  9
+  2  2  2  1
  ▢  ▢  ▢  ▢
```

(h)
```
   1  3  2  4
+  3  4  5  8
  ▢  ▢  ▢  ▢
```

2 Solve and fill in the blanks.

Jacob took 2328 steps to get to school in the morning.

He took 1235 fewer steps than Elliott took.

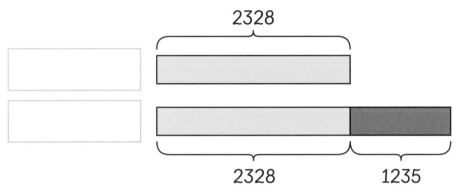

(a) How many steps did Elliott take to get to school in the morning?

Elliott took ☐ steps to get to school in the morning.

(b) How many steps did Elliott and Jacob take altogether?

Elliott and Jacob took ☐ steps altogether.

Adding with renaming (part 2)

Starter

Sam's high score on the Mega-Speed game is 7485 points.
Ruby's high score beat Sam's high score by 1236 points.
How many points did Ruby score on the Mega-Speed game?

Example

7485

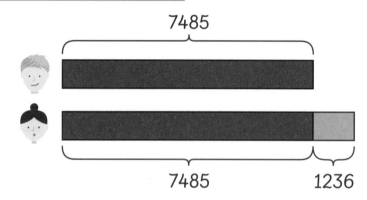

7485   1236

We need to add 7485 and 1236 to find Ruby's high score.

Step 1   Add the ones.
5 ones and 6 ones = 11 ones
Rename the ones.
11 ones = 1 ten and 1 one

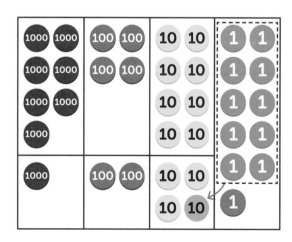

$$
\begin{array}{r}
7 \quad 4 \quad {}^{1}8 \quad 5 \\
+ \; 1 \quad 2 \quad 3 \quad 6 \\
\hline
1
\end{array}
$$

16

Step 2 Add the tens.

8 tens + 3 tens + 1 ten = 12 tens

Rename the tens.

12 tens = 1 hundred and 2 tens

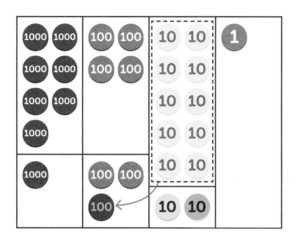

$$
\begin{array}{r}
7 \;\; {}^{1}4 \;\; {}^{1}8 \;\; 5 \\
+ \;\; 1 \;\; 2 \;\; 3 \;\; 6 \\
\hline
2 \;\; 1
\end{array}
$$

Step 3 Add the hundreds.

4 hundreds + 2 hundreds + 1 hundred = 7 hundreds

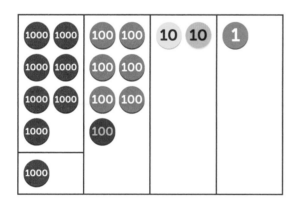

$$
\begin{array}{r}
7 \;\; {}^{1}4 \;\; {}^{1}8 \;\; 5 \\
+ \;\; 1 \;\; 2 \;\; 3 \;\; 6 \\
\hline
7 \;\; 2 \;\; 1
\end{array}
$$

Step 4 Add the thousands.

7 thousands + 1 thousand = 8 thousands

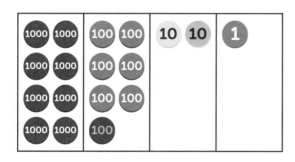

$$
\begin{array}{r}
7 \;\; {}^{1}4 \;\; {}^{t}8 \;\; 5 \\
+ \;\; 1 \;\; 2 \;\; 3 \;\; 6 \\
\hline
8 \;\; 7 \;\; 2 \;\; 1
\end{array}
$$

7485 + 1236 = 8721

Ruby scored 8721 points on the Mega-Speed game.

1 Add.

(a)
```
    4  2  4  9
+   2  6  8  5
  ┌──┬──┬──┬──┐
  │  │  │  │  │
  └──┴──┴──┴──┘
```

(b)
```
    3  1  8  2
+   3  4  1  8
  ┌──┬──┬──┬──┐
  │  │  │  │  │
  └──┴──┴──┴──┘
```

(c)
```
    8  3  6  6
+   1  3  8  7
  ┌──┬──┬──┬──┐
  │  │  │  │  │
  └──┴──┴──┴──┘
```

(d)
```
    7  3  9  3
+   1  4  9  5
  ┌──┬──┬──┬──┐
  │  │  │  │  │
  └──┴──┴──┴──┘
```

(e)
```
    1  0  7  5
+   8  6  7  8
  ┌──┬──┬──┬──┐
  │  │  │  │  │
  └──┴──┴──┴──┘
```

(f)
```
    4  7  9  9
+   4  0  8  9
  ┌──┬──┬──┬──┐
  │  │  │  │  │
  └──┴──┴──┴──┘
```

(g)
```
    1  1  3  4
+   2  1  6  7
  ┌──┬──┬──┬──┐
  │  │  │  │  │
  └──┴──┴──┴──┘
```

(h)
```
    2  1  5  6
+   1  1  4  5
  ┌──┬──┬──┬──┐
  │  │  │  │  │
  └──┴──┴──┴──┘
```

2 Solve and fill in the blanks.

The music teacher bought a new drum kit for £3299 for the school. He also bought some guitars and amps that cost £2076 more than the drum kit.

£ [   ]

drum kit [   ]

guitars and amps [   ]

£ [   ]   £ [   ]

(a) How much did the music teacher spend on guitars and amps?

[   ]

The music teacher spent £ [   ] on guitars and amps.

(b) How much did the music teacher spend in total?

[   ]

The music teacher spent £ [   ] in total.

Adding with renaming (part 3)

Starter

On Wednesday, an aeroplane left London and flew 6374 km to Chicago.
It then left Chicago and flew 2997 km to San Francisco.

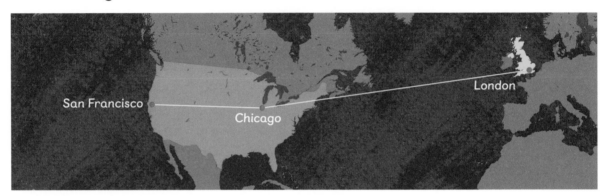

How far did the aeroplane fly on Wednesday?

Example

Add 6374 and 2997.

Step 1   Add the ones.
4 ones and 7 ones = 11 ones
Rename the ones.
11 ones = 1 ten and 1 one

$$
\begin{array}{r}
6 \quad 3 \quad {}^{1}7 \quad 4 \\
+ \; 2 \quad 9 \quad 9 \quad 7 \\
\hline
1
\end{array}
$$

Step 2   Add the tens.
7 tens + 9 tens + 1 ten = 17 tens
Rename the tens.
17 tens = 1 hundred and 7 tens

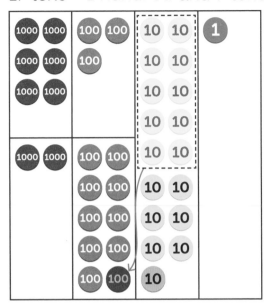

$$
\begin{array}{r}
6\ \ ^{1}3\ \ ^{1}7\ \ 4 \\
+\ \ 2\ \ \ 9\ \ \ 9\ \ \ 7 \\
\hline
7\ \ \ 1 \\
\hline
\end{array}
$$

Step 3   Add the hundreds.
3 hundreds + 9 hundreds + 1 hundred = 13 hundreds

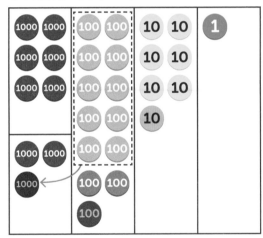

$$
\begin{array}{r}
^{1}6\ \ ^{1}3\ \ ^{1}7\ \ 4 \\
+\ \ 2\ \ \ 9\ \ \ 9\ \ \ 7 \\
\hline
3\ \ \ 7\ \ \ 1 \\
\hline
\end{array}
$$

Step 4   Add the thousands.
6 thousands + 2 thousands + 1 thousand = 9 thousands

$$
\begin{array}{r}
^{1}6\ \ ^{1}3\ \ ^{1}7\ \ 4 \\
+\ \ 2\ \ \ 9\ \ \ 9\ \ \ 7 \\
\hline
9\ \ \ 3\ \ \ 7\ \ \ 1 \\
\hline
\end{array}
$$

6374 + 2997 = 9371

The aeroplane flew 9371 km on Wednesday.

1 Add.

(a)
```
    5   5   3   8
+   2   7   8   5
  [   ][   ][   ][   ]
```

(b)
```
    6   8   9   3
+   1   4   7   9
  [   ][   ][   ][   ]
```

(c)
```
    7   3   8   6
+   1   9   3   7
  [   ][   ][   ][   ]
```

(d)
```
    2   7   9   3
+   5   8   4   9
  [   ][   ][   ][   ]
```

(e)
```
    4   4   5   8
+   4   8   6   5
  [   ][   ][   ][   ]
```

(f)
```
    1   9   9   9
+   1   2   1   1
  [   ][   ][   ][   ]
```

(g)
```
    3   1   2   1
+   5   9   7   0
  [   ][   ][   ][   ]
```

(h)
```
    2   2   3   5
+   3   8   8   5
  [   ][   ][   ][   ]
```

2 On Saturday, 4797 people attended a football match at the stadium.
On Sunday, 4658 people attended a music concert at the stadium.
How many people in total attended the two events at the stadium?

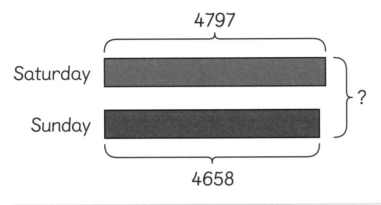

people in total attended the two events at the stadium.

Subtracting without renaming

Starter

At the last count, the Serengeti National Park in Tanzania had 2888 wild lions. The Kruger National Park in South Africa had 1630 wild lions.

How many more lions were there in the Serengeti National Park than in the Kruger National Park?

Example

We need to find the difference. That means we need to subtract 1630 from 2888.

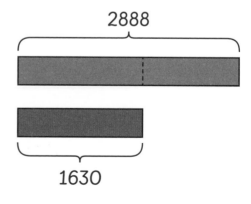

2888

1630

24

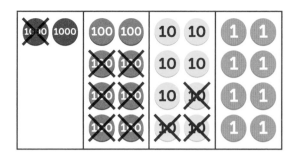

Step 1   Subtract the ones.
Step 2   Subtract the tens.
Step 3   Subtract the hundreds.
Step 4   Subtract the thousands.

2888 − 1630 = 1258
There are 1258 more lions in the
Serengeti National Park than there
are in the Kruger National Park.

```
    2   8   8   8
−   1   6   3   0
─────────────────
    1   2   5   8
```

1   Subtract.

(a)
```
    7   7   5   2
−   5   3   4   1
─────────────────
  [  ][  ][  ][  ]
```

(b)
```
    8   9   9   4
−   2   3   7   4
─────────────────
  [  ][  ][  ][  ]
```

(c)
```
    9   4   5   1
−   6   3   4   0
─────────────────
  [  ][  ][  ][  ]
```

(d)
```
    5   8   4   5
−   2   5   1   2
─────────────────
  [  ][  ][  ][  ]
```

2 Blundell Park football stadium can hold 9546 fans.
Deva Stadium can hold 5126 fans.
How many fewer fans does Deva Stadium hold than Blundell Park?

9546

5126

Deva Stadium holds ⬚ fewer fans than Blundell Park.

3 There were 9466 buffalo in the Masai Mara National Reserve in Kenya in 2017 and 7342 buffalo in 2014.
How many fewer buffalo were there in 2014?

There were ⬚ fewer buffalo in 2014.

4 In 2017, there were 2498 elephants in the Masai Mara National Reserve in Kenya. In 2014, there were 1443 elephants.

1443

2014

2017

2498

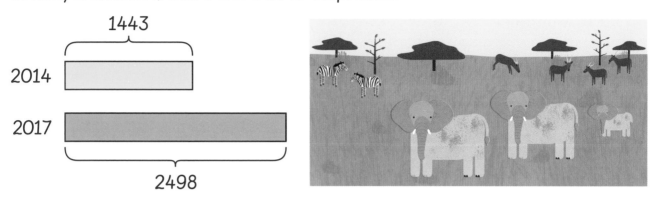

How many more elephants were there in 2017 than in 2014?

There were ☐ more elephants in 2017 than in 2014.

Subtracting with renaming (part 1)

Starter

Mount Makalu is in the Himalayan mountain range.
It is the fifth highest mountain in the world and is 8481 m tall.
Mount Nanga Parbat is also in the Himalayan
mountain range.
It is the ninth highest mountain in the world at 8125 m tall.

What is the difference in height between the two mountains?

Example

We need to subtract to find the difference.

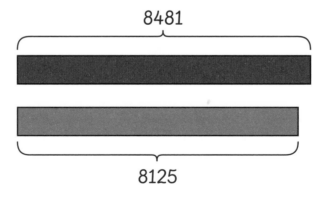

8481

8125

28

Subtract 8125 from 8481.

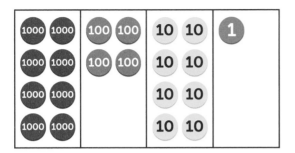

There are not enough ones.

	8	4	8	1
−	8	1	2	5

	8	4	$^7\cancel{8}$	$^{11}\cancel{1}$
−	8	1	2	5

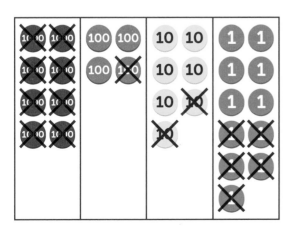

	8	4	$^7\cancel{8}$	$^{11}\cancel{1}$
−	8	1	2	5
		3	5	6

8481

8 thousands	4 hundreds	⁷ 8̸ tens	¹¹ 1̸ ones
− 8 thousands	− 1 hundreds	− 2 tens	− 5 ones
0 thousands	3 hundreds	5 tens	6 ones

8481 − 8125 = 356

The difference in height between the
two mountains is 356 m.

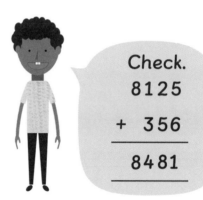

Check.

8125
+ 356
―――――
8481

Practice

1 Subtract.

(a)
```
    8  5  8  4
 -  5  4  6  9
 ――――――――――――
 [  ][  ][  ][  ]
 ――――――――――――
```

(b)
```
    7  3  7  1
 -  3  2  4  3
 ――――――――――――
 [  ][  ][  ][  ]
 ――――――――――――
```

(c)
```
    7  4  8  3
 -  6  3  5  6
 ――――――――――――
 [  ][  ][  ][  ]
 ――――――――――――
```

(d)
```
    5  6  7  5
 -  3  3  4  8
 ――――――――――――
 [  ][  ][  ][  ]
 ――――――――――――
```

(e)
```
    6   5   7   4
–   2   2   3   9
  [   ][   ][   ][   ]
```

(f)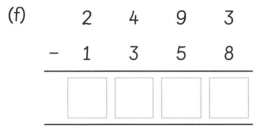
```
    2   4   9   3
–   1   3   5   8
  [   ][   ][   ][   ]
```

2 Ravi and his family fly from Manchester to Los Angeles.
The distance is 5281 miles.
After flying 3109 miles the aeroplane is over Montréal.

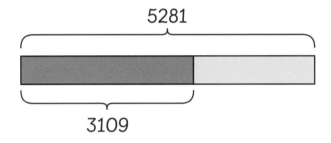

5281

3109

How much further do they need to fly to reach Los Angeles?

Ravi and his family still need to fly [   ] miles to reach Los Angeles.

Subtracting with renaming (part 2)

Starter

The longest passenger train ever operated was in Australia. It was 1097 m long. The longest freight train ever operated was also in Australia. It was 7242 m long.

What is the difference in metres between the two trains?

Example

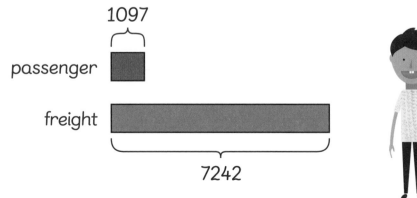

We subtract to find the difference.

Subtract 1097 from 7242.

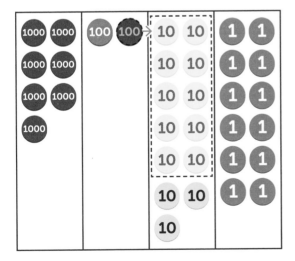

There are not enough ones.

```
    7   2   4   2
-   1   0   9   7
_____

_____
```

There are not enough tens.

```
             3   12
    7   2   4   2
-   1   0   9   7
_____

_____
```

```
        1   13   12
    7   2   4   2
-   1   0   9   7
_____

_____
```

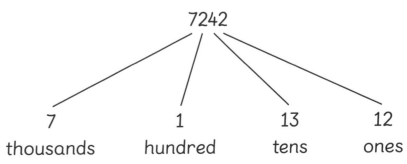

7242

7 thousands   1 hundred   13 tens   12 ones

$$\begin{array}{r} 7\ \overset{1}{\cancel{2}}\ \overset{13}{\cancel{4}}\ \overset{12}{\cancel{2}} \\ -\ 1\ 0\ 9\ 7 \\ \hline 6\ 1\ 4\ 5 \end{array}$$

Check.

6145 + 1097 = 7242

7242 − 1097 = 6145

The difference between the two trains is 6145 m.

Practice

1 Subtract.

(a)
$$\begin{array}{r} 4\ 3\ 3\ 1 \\ -\ 2\ 1\ 4\ 5 \\ \hline \square\ \square\ \square\ \square \end{array}$$

(b)
$$\begin{array}{r} 7\ 3\ 1\ 4 \\ -\ 5\ 1\ 8\ 6 \\ \hline \square\ \square\ \square\ \square \end{array}$$

(c)
$$\begin{array}{r} 9\ 4\ 9\ 1 \\ -\ 6\ 3\ 9\ 6 \\ \hline \square\ \square\ \square\ \square \end{array}$$

(d)
$$\begin{array}{r} 6\ 7\ 1\ 2 \\ -\ 3\ 6\ 1\ 7 \\ \hline \square\ \square\ \square\ \square \end{array}$$

2 Jacob walked 6756 steps on Monday and 8412 steps on Tuesday.
On Wednesday he walked 7924 steps.

Monday	6756
Tuesday	8412
Wednesday	7924

(a) How many more steps did Jacob walk on Tuesday than on Monday?

Jacob walked _____ more steps on Tuesday than on Monday.

(b) How many fewer steps did Jacob walk on Monday than on Wednesday?

Jacob walked _____ fewer steps on Monday than on Wednesday.

Subtracting with renaming (part 3)

Starter

The usual price for this piano is £8000.
How much does the piano cost if you buy it today?

Example

We need to subtract 2215 from 8000 to find the price.

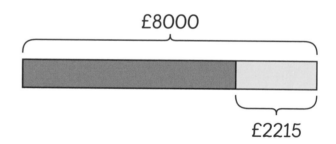

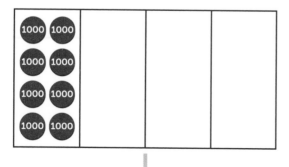

8000

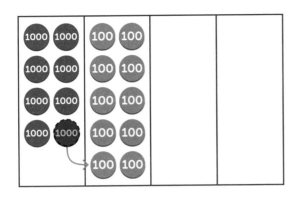

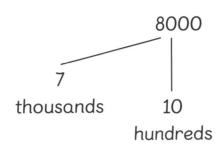

8000

7
thousands

10
hundreds

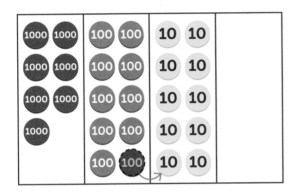

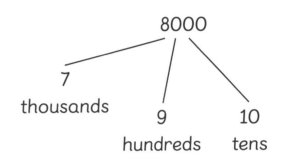

8000

7
thousands

9
hundreds

10
tens

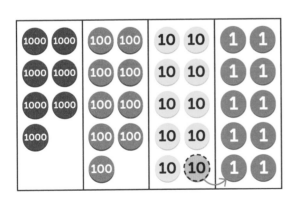

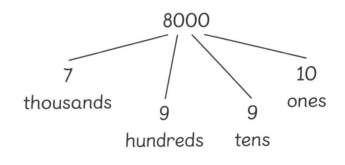

8000

7
thousands

9
hundreds

9
tens

10
ones

$$\begin{array}{r}
{}^{7}\cancel{8}\ {}^{9}\cancel{0}\ {}^{9}\cancel{0}\ {}^{10}\cancel{0} \\
-\ 2\ \ 2\ \ 1\ \ 5 \\
\hline
5\ \ 7\ \ 8\ \ 5 \\
\hline
\end{array}$$

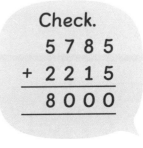

Check.

$$\begin{array}{r}
5\ 7\ 8\ 5 \\
+\ 2\ 2\ 1\ 5 \\
\hline
8\ 0\ 0\ 0 \\
\hline
\end{array}$$

1 Subtract.

(a)
```
    3   2   2   3
 -  1   7   2   5
  _____
  [ ] [ ] [ ] [ ]
  _____
```

(b)
```
    4   6   0   0
 -  2   8   4   3
  _____
  [ ] [ ] [ ] [ ]
  _____
```

(c)
```
    8   0   0   0
 -  7   8   5   4
  _____
  [ ] [ ] [ ] [ ]
  _____
```

(d)
```
    9   0   0   0
 -  7   6   2   1
  _____
  [ ] [ ] [ ] [ ]
  _____
```

(e)
```
    6   0   0   0
 -  5   3   2   5
  _____
  [ ] [ ] [ ] [ ]
  _____
```

(f)
```
    4   0   0   0
 -  3   4   6   7
  _____
  [ ] [ ] [ ] [ ]
  _____
```

(g)
```
    5   0   0   0
 -  2   3   8   6
  _____
  [ ] [ ] [ ] [ ]
  _____
```

(h)
```
    3   0   0   0
 -  1   9   9   9
  _____
  [ ] [ ] [ ] [ ]
  _____
```

2 A stadium seats 8000 people for a concert.
4723 tickets have been sold so far.
How many tickets are left to sell?

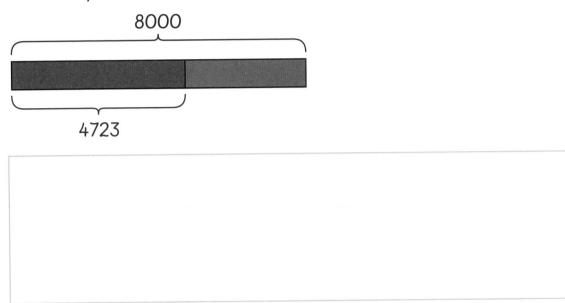

There are [ ] tickets left to sell.

3 Emma wants to walk 7000 steps a day to be healthy.
So far today she has walked 2884 steps.
How many more steps must Emma walk today?

7000

2884

Emma must walk [ ] more steps today.

Review and challenge

1 Write the numbers in words.

6752

8253

6570

1013

2 Write the words in numerals.

two thousand, four hundred and ninety-two

one thousand, two hundred and eighteen

five thousand, five hundred and ninety

four thousand and forty-three

3 Put the numbers in order from smallest to greatest.

(a) 9953, 4812, 6955, 7988

☐ , ☐ , ☐ , ☐

(b) 3013, 3103, 3310, 3130

☐ , ☐ , ☐ , ☐

4 Put the numbers in order from greatest to smallest.

(a) 2781, 2530, 3181, 2978

☐ , ☐ , ☐ , ☐

(b) 5432, 5342, 5423, 5324

☐ , ☐ , ☐ , ☐

5 Add.

(a)
```
   7  3  2  3
+  2  3  3  4
  ☐  ☐  ☐  ☐
```

(b)
```
   4  0  4  8
+  3  1  3  4
  ☐  ☐  ☐  ☐
```

(c)
```
   3  1  2  5
+  4  7  7  9
  ☐  ☐  ☐  ☐
```

(d)
```
   5  8  6  3
+  2  4  6  8
  ☐  ☐  ☐  ☐
```

(e)
```
   7  8  7  5
+  1  1  9  8
  ☐  ☐  ☐  ☐
```

(f)
```
   3  5  7  1
+  1  4  2  9
  ☐  ☐  ☐  ☐
```

6 Subtract.

(a)
```
    3  1  7  7
 -  1  1  2  1
   _____
   [  ][  ][  ][  ]
   _____
```

(b)
```
    6  5  9  5
 -  1  2  7  8
   _____
   [  ][  ][  ][  ]
   _____
```

(c)
```
    7  6  5  7
 -  7  3  6  8
   _____
   [  ][  ][  ][  ]
   _____
```

(d)
```
    4  2  5  5
 -  2  6  8  7
   _____
   [  ][  ][  ][  ]
   _____
```

(e)
```
    6  0  0  0
 -  3  9  6  3
   _____
   [  ][  ][  ][  ]
   _____
```

(f)
```
    8  0  0  0
 -  5  7  9  4
   _____
   [  ][  ][  ][  ]
   _____
```

7 Elliott and Ruby finish playing a board game and want to play again.
They need to share all the play money equally to start the game over.
Ruby gives Elliott £625 of her play money.
They now have the same amount.

(a) How much more play money did Ruby have than Elliott at the end
of the last game?

Ruby had £ ⬚ more play money than Elliott had at the

end of the last game.

(b) At the end of the second game, Ruby has £1285 in play money
and Elliott has £1715.
How much money does Elliott need to give back to Ruby so that
they have the same amount of play money?

Elliott needs to give Ruby £ ⬚ so that they have the

same amount of play money.

8 On Friday, 3597 children visited the Science Museum.
On Saturday, 2489 more children visited the Science Museum than visited on Friday.
On Sunday, 1287 fewer children visited the Science Museum than on Saturday.

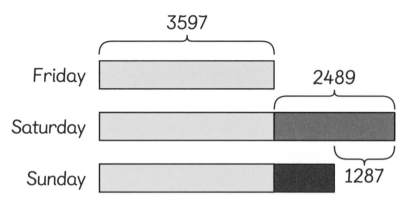

(a) How many children visited the Science Museum on Saturday?

children visited the Science Museum on Saturday.

(b) How many children visited the Science Museum on Sunday?

children visited the Science Museum on Sunday.

(c) How many children visited the Science Museum on Saturday and Sunday in total?

children visited the Science Museum on Saturday and Sunday in total.

Answers

Page 5   **2** seven thousand, five hundred and forty-six, 7546   **3** four thousand, three hundred and sixty-seven, 4367
            4 one thousand, seven hundred and thirty-six, 1736

Page 7   **1 (a)** 1298, 3598, 4680, 5762   **(b)** 3778, 3779, 3784, 3893   **2 (a)** 4012, 3112, 2956, 2875   **(b)** 5601, 5543, 5542, 5479

Page 9   **1 (a)** 7879   **(b)** 9989   **(c)** 8348   **(d)** 9939   **(e)** 9999   **(f)** 8888

Page 10   **2 (a)** The driving distance from Vancouver to Moncton is 5943 km.   **(b)** The total driving distance from Vancouver to Mirabel is 6978 km.

Page 11   **3 (a)**

5	4	3	3
+ 4	4	3	2
9	8	6	5

(b)

5	4	3	2
+ 4	4	3	3
9	8	6	5

(c)

2	3	4	5
+ 3	3	4	4
5	6	8	9

(d)

2	3	4	4
+ 3	3	4	5
5	6	8	9

Page 14   **1 (a)**

3	2	¹4	7
+ 2	5	4	6
5	7	9	3

(b)

1	4	¹3	5
+ 5	3	5	6
6	7	9	1

(c)

5	4	¹3	6
+ 1	0	2	8
6	4	6	4

(d)

1	1	¹0	6
+ 2	1	5	6
3	2	6	2

(e)

8	2	¹6	1
+ 1	6	2	9
9	8	9	0

(f)

1	3	¹3	9
+ 8	5	5	1
9	8	9	0

(g)

1	1	¹1	9
+ 2	2	2	1
3	3	4	0

(h)

1	3	¹2	4
+ 3	4	5	8
4	7	8	2

Page 15   **2**

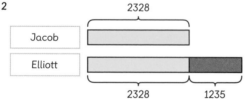

                                   (a) Elliott took 3563 steps to get to school in the morning.
                                     (b) Elliott and Jacob took 5891 steps altogether.

Page 18   **1 (a)**

4	¹2	¹4	9
+ 2	6	8	5
6	9	3	4

(b)

3	¹1	¹8	2
+ 3	4	1	8
6	6	0	0

(c)

8	¹3	¹6	6
+ 1	3	8	7
9	7	5	3

(d)

7	¹3	9	3
+ 1	4	9	5
8	8	8	8

(e)

1	¹0	¹7	5
+ 8	6	7	8
9	7	5	3

(f)

4	¹7	¹9	9
+ 4	0	8	9
8	8	8	8

(g)

1	¹1	¹3	4
+ 2	1	6	7
3	3	0	1

(h)

2	¹1	¹5	6
+ 1	1	4	5
3	3	0	1

Page 19   **2**

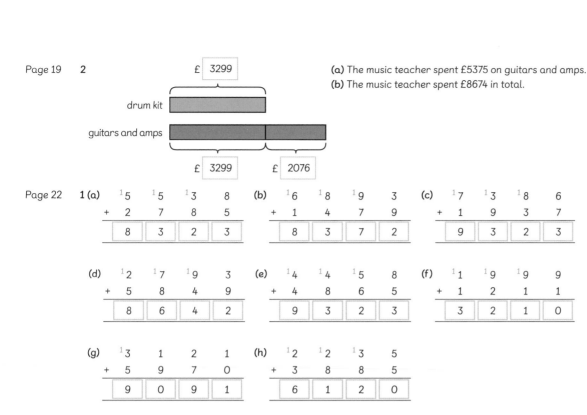

(a) The music teacher spent £5375 on guitars and amps.
(b) The music teacher spent £8674 in total.

Page 22   **1 (a)**

	¹5	¹5	¹3	8
+	2	7	8	5
	8	3	2	3

(b)

	¹6	¹8	¹9	3
+	1	4	7	9
	8	3	7	2

(c)

	¹7	¹3	¹8	6
+	1	9	3	7
	9	3	2	3

(d)

	¹2	¹7	¹9	3
+	5	8	4	9
	8	6	4	2

(e)

	¹4	¹4	¹5	8
+	4	8	6	5
	9	3	2	3

(f)

	¹1	¹9	¹9	9
+	1	2	1	1
	3	2	1	0

(g)

	¹3	1	2	1
+	5	9	7	0
	9	0	9	1

(h)

	¹2	¹2	¹3	5
+	3	8	8	5
	6	1	2	0

Page 23   **2** 9455 people in total attended the two events at the stadium.

Page 25   **1 (a)** 2411 **(b)** 6620 **(c)** 3111 **(d)** 3333

Page 26   **2** Deva Stadium holds 4420 fewer fans than Blundell Park. **3** There were 2124 fewer buffalo in 2014.

Page 27   **4** There were 1055 more elephants in 2017 than in 2014.

Page 30   **1 (a)**

	8	5	⁷8̸	¹⁴4̸
−	5	4	6	9
	3	1	1	5

(b)

	7	3	⁶7̸	¹¹1̸
−	3	2	4	3
	4	1	2	8

(c)

	7	4	⁷8̸	¹³3̸
−	6	3	5	6
	1	1	2	7

(d)

	5	6	⁶7̸	¹⁵5̸
−	3	3	4	8
	2	3	2	7

Page 31   **(e)**

	6	5	⁶7̸	¹⁴4̸
−	2	2	3	9
	4	3	3	5

(f)

	2	4	⁸9̸	¹³3̸
−	1	3	5	8
	1	1	3	5

2 Ravi and his family still need to fly 2172 miles to reach Los Angeles.

Page 34   **1 (a)**

	4	²3̸	¹²3̸	¹¹1̸
−	2	1	4	5
	2	1	8	6

(b)

	7	²3̸	¹⁰1̸	¹⁴4̸
−	5	1	8	6
	2	1	2	8

(c)

	9	³4̸	¹⁸9̸	¹¹1̸
−	6	3	9	6
	3	0	9	5

(d)

	6	⁶7̸	¹⁰1̸	¹²2̸
−	3	6	1	7
	3	0	9	5

Page 35   **2 (a)** Jacob walked 1656 more steps on Tuesday than on Monday. **(b)** Jacob walked 1168 fewer steps on Monday than on Wednesday.

47

Answers continued

Page 38 **1 (a)**

	²3̸	¹¹2̸	¹¹2̸	¹³3̸
−	1	7	2	5
	1	4	9	8

(b)

	³4̸	¹⁵6̸	⁹0̸	¹⁰0̸
−	2	8	4	3
	1	7	5	7

(c)

	⁷8̸	⁹0̸	⁹0̸	¹⁰0̸
−	7	8	5	4
		1	4	6

(d)

	⁸9̸	⁹0̸	⁹0̸	¹⁰0̸
−	7	6	2	1
	1	3	7	9

(e)

	⁵6̸	⁹0̸	⁹0̸	¹⁰0̸
−	5	3	2	5
		6	7	5

(f)

	³4̸	⁹0̸	⁹0̸	¹⁰0̸
−	3	4	6	7
		5	3	3

(g)

	⁴5̸	⁹0̸	⁹0̸	¹⁰0̸
−	2	3	8	6
	2	6	1	4

(h)

	²3̸	⁹0̸	⁹0̸	¹⁰0̸
−	1	9	9	9
	1	0	0	1

Page 39 **2** There are 3277 tickets left to sell. **3** Emma must walk 4116 more steps today.

Page 40 **1** six thousand, seven hundred and fifty-two; eight thousand, two hundred and fifty-three; six thousand, five hundred and seventy; one thousand and thirteen **2** 2492; 1218; 5590; 4043

Page 41 **3 (a)** 4812, 6955, 7988, 9953 **(b)** 3013, 3103, 3130, 3310 **4 (a)** 3181, 2978, 2781, 2530 **(b)** 5432, 5423, 5342, 5324

5 (a)

	7	3	2	3
+	2	3	3	4
	9	6	5	7

(b)

	4	0	¹4	8
+	3	1	3	4
	7	1	8	2

(c)

	3	¹1	¹2	5
+	4	7	7	9
	7	9	0	4

(d)

	¹5	¹8	¹6	3
+	2	4	6	8
	8	3	3	1

(e)

	¹7	¹8	¹7	5
+	1	1	9	8
	9	0	7	3

(f)

	¹3	¹5	¹7	1
+	1	4	2	9
	5	0	0	0

Page 42 **6 (a)**

	3	1	7	7
−	1	1	2	1
	2	0	5	6

(b)

	6	5	⁸9̸	¹⁵5̸
−	1	2	7	8
	5	3	1	7

(c)

	7	⁵6̸	¹⁴5̸	¹⁷7̸
−	7	3	6	8
		2	8	9

(d)

	³4̸	¹¹2̸	¹⁴5̸	¹⁵5̸
−	2	6	8	7
	1	5	6	8

(e)

	⁵6̸	⁹0̸	⁹0̸	¹⁰0̸
−	3	9	6	3
	2	0	3	7

(f)

	⁷8̸	⁹0̸	⁹0̸	¹⁰0̸
−	5	7	9	4
	2	2	0	6

Page 43 **7 (a)**

		6	¹2	5
+		6	2	5
	1	2	5	0

625 + 625 = 1250
Ruby had £1250 more play money than Elliott at the end of the last game.

(b)

	1	⁶7̸	¹¹1̸	5
−	1	2	8	5
		4	3	0

1715 − 1285 = 430
430 ÷ 2 = 215
Elliott needs to give Ruby £215 so that they have the same amount of play money.

Page 44 **8 (a)** 6086 children visited the Science Museum on Saturday.

Page 45 **(b)** 4799 children visited the Science Museum on Sunday.
(c) 10885 children visited the Science Museum on Saturday and Sunday in total.